STEP
INTO YOUR
PURPOSE

A life without purpose is a life not lived

STEP
INTO YOUR
PURPOSE

Discover Your Life's True Purpose & Meaning

JERRY BONSU

Published in France by VICTORY LIFE MEDIA an imprint of JBM

JERRY BONSU MINISTRIES
http://www.jerrybonsu.org

VLM books may be ordered through booksellers or by visiting www.jerrybonsu.org. VLM Speakers Bureau provides a wide range of authors for speaking events. To find out more, email us: victorylifemedia@gmail.com.

French National Library-in-Publication Data
Dépôt légal: 01/2017

Cover design by VLM
Printed in the United States of America
ISBN: 978-2-9541960-8-4

For further information or permission, contact us on the Internet:

VICTORY LIFE MEDIA "Empowering our Generation for the next Generation" www.victorylifemedia.com.

DEDICATION

I dedicate this book to my family, to my friends, to my followers, to my leaders.

CONTENTS

INTRODUCTION

Many of us have fallen into a space in our lives where we have strayed away from our true-life purpose (calling). You may be in this place right now, where you have acknowledged that life did not serve up your desired outcomes and you are ready to do something about it.

Let me affirm that there comes a critical time when subconsciously resisting our true calling is no longer an option. We reach a point of critical mass when the life situations we are currently facing make us feel so unfilled we are ready to make dramatic and significant changes.

You might not have the exact vision of what you want; it might be a feeling that something greater, happier and bigger is possible for your life.

With all this realization that your life kind of sucks in its current status... You still may be caught in a state of resisting your calling and resisting your purpose because you are used to the old behaviors that got you into this in the first place. You are stuck with a life you don't like but don't know what to do about creating something new... wondered whether you can actually move into the full purpose and destiny God has for you.

Friend, I HAVE GOOD NEWS! It is normal if your burning desire is to accomplish something greater than yourself, because God does nothing without a purpose. We are all call to greatness. Each person is created by God for a unique and important purpose. That is why we all have an inner yearning to find our true-life purpose. We want to know why we are on earth. We desire to know our unique PURPOSE. We ask ourselves, "What is God's will for my life?"

I remember when I was in senior high school; I was faced with having to know what God's will for my life was. Even though I knew that God was preparing me for a mission (great things). I hadn't thought about it much before that, because for fifteen years, I was just a student. But at that point, I needed to know if I was supposed to go to university or what path God wanted me to take.

I believe that our existence is evidence that our purpose is necessary. That is why it is so crucial for you to take time to discover God's intention for creating you. Dr. Myles Munroe once said, "The greatest tragedy in life isn't death but living a life without a purpose."

A life without a purpose is a life without a **destination**. It's like a boat adrift on the ocean, there is no telling where you might end up. With no direction to your life, you will be moved by random feelings and emotions into any harbor.

"Purpose Driven" author, Pastor Rick Warren said, "God formed every creature on this planet with a special area of expertise. Some animals run, some hop, some swim, some burrow, and some fly. Each has a particular role to play based on the way they were shaped by God. The same is true with humans. Each of us is uniquely designed, or shaped, to do certain things."

I wrote this book to remind you that God created you for a unique purpose and you are blessed with the power to achieve it. Your birth was no mistake or mishap, and your life is no fluke of nature. Your parents may not have planned you, but God did. He was not at all surprised by your birth. In fact, He expected it.

In Jeremiah 1:5a, God said, "I knew you before I formed you in your mother's womb. Before you were born I set you apart." What does God mean, "Before I formed you in the womb I knew you, and before you were born I set you apart?"

Throughout the Scripture (the Bible), God sets apart people for Himself and His purposes. It is vital for you to know that you are special to God. You are part of a chosen generation, a royal priesthood, a peculiar people chosen by God to show His glory to the world.

Beloved, there is something phenomenal you were born to accomplish. What is more, God has equipped you with the gifts and talents to fulfill it. The truth is, you have a glorious destiny. You were not created to barely make it. You were fashioned in the image of God, and suited for a great purpose. What you have inside of you is more than gift, it is a solution!

The world is looking (waiting) for someone with answers. Your neighbors need to see that there is someone who has ACCESS to a power greater than that which exists in the world. The creation are waiting for your manifestation! Yes, the world is waiting for you to share your gifts, talents, and abilities with them! The question is, are you ready?

You see, great things don't happen by chance or accident, they happen by conscious STEPS taken for actualization. You have great things in you but those things will not see the light of the day except by manifesting them... I truly believe that when you step out, you will see the fruit you were created to bear.

We have a purpose and God has a plan. He has a plan to bring us into greatness. This book is very dear to my heart. In it I have tried to share with you what I believe will help you to actualise your destiny... and walk in your God-given purpose. Every single word you read this day is from a heart taken over by God, to speak to you and to declare to you the mind of God, that the time for you to receive every good and perfect gift from God has come.

I pray that through this book you will be encouraged and blessed—knowing that you are here on this earth for a great purpose. It is also my prayer that by the time you finish reading this life-changing book, God reveal Himself to you and make His purpose for your life known to you.

Are you ready to step into your **PURPOSE**? Ready to step into God's great plan for your life? Then let's go!!!

"The two most important days in your life are the day you are born and the day you find out why."

Mark Twain

Chapter
ONE
Identity

*"If you don't know your identity,
other people will identify you."*

Ashanti Proverb

Who **Am** I?... is an arresting title. It is one of the most relevant questions humanity asks. And it is a question many people struggle to answer.

Have you ever thought about who you are? What you stand for? I'm not talking about your roles or social identities. Yes, you can be a friend, brother, sister, husband, wife, father, mother, son, daughter, employee, all at the same time, but these are just an aspect of you. They don't represent who you fundamentally are inside.

Knowing yourself and growing into your true identity is priceless. Without identity there is no way to move in any direction with any sense of purpose. No **identity** equals No **purpose** — No **purpose** equals No **vision** (special revelation). And without VISION or a revelation of God we are unrestrained and left to ourselves.

So what is **identity**?... Identity is defined as "the collective aspect of the set of characteristics by which a thing is definitively recognizable or known," It can also defined as "the quality or condition of being the same as something else." According to Yourdictionary.com; "It is who you are, the way you think about YOURSELF, the way you are viewed by the world and the characteristics that define you.

To know your identity (Who you are) is to know your purpose, your values, your visions, your motivations, your goals and your beliefs. Not as what you have been told by others, but what you have discovered in the Word of God for yourself— it is about letting God transform you into who He wants you to be.

You will never discover who you are by looking inside yourself or listening to what others say. If you want to know who you are, look at God. Your true identity is who God says you are. That is why it is important to never accept the definition of anybody about you but God's definition of who you are.

Don't let people define you! Don't let your *self-perception* change according to who is around. Don't let your self-esteem depend on the number of likes, re-tweets or comments you get on social media. You are so much more than that. You are enough and important. You are valuable to God! Never let your race, gender or position define and determine who you are and what you can do. Your identity is found in CHRIST, and in Christ alone!

Friend, what I want you to realize is that, you are more than other people's opinion! You are more than what you think you are! You are more than your job, your degree, your bank account, the car you drive, your relationship status or your past.

You are who God says you are!

You have what God says you have!

You can do what God says you can!

So, don't let the devil steal your identity by telling you what God has not said about you. Thieves don't break into empty houses. The enemy knows that you are VALUABLE to the Kingdom of God that is why he keeps attacking you. The devil is not after your destiny! he is after your identity! If you don't know who you are… satan will use you to be who he want you to be.

The Bible says, you have been fearfully and wonderfully made in the image of God. You are chosen by God… with purpose, for purpose, on purpose! Your IDENTITY is rooted in Christ, the unchanging Creator of each and every soul. You have God's DNA in you! The Lord says, "I will be a Father to you, and you will be my sons and daughters." (See 2 Corinthians 6:18).

You are not an accident. (See Jeremiah 1:5) Your conception might be unplanned but God fixed you into His plan. You have been made the way you are to be SUITABLE for accomplishing your God-given purpose. You are who you are because God took you out of Himself. So if you want to know your identity, you must look at the Creator, not the creation.

When you come to the realization that who you are in God is your strength and confidence, you won't let anyone tear you down and tell you your identity. They don't set labels on you, God does. And He calls you His child. Yes! God — the Creator, Sustainer, and Giver of Life… calls us His children! The Bible declares that,

"See what great love the Father has lavished on us, that we should be called children of God! And that is what we are! The reason the world does not know us is that it did not know him."

1 John 3:1

In this season of your life, you must identify with your new identity (child of God)! You must think and talk about yourself how God (the Father) talks about you! As I have mentioned earlier, this *world* will try to label and define you, but only God can tell you who you are. He knows our identities perfectly. And I believe He wants to help us know ourselves as well.

On the other hand, satan (the accuser of the brethren) doesn't want us to know our identity. As a matter of fact, he is an identity thief and he is working full time. his goal is to rob you of your identity, and to stop your influence! But glory be to God that we are no longer defeated by satan. Victory is our identity because victory is who God is.

Friend, when you discover who God is, you discover who you are. And when you discover who you are, you no longer have to struggle with the insecurity and self-promotion that define much of society. You no longer have to strain to measure up, to qualify. You are free to be yourself! Free to be YOU!

Free to tap into the fatherhood of God through our Lord Jesus... and you will know true love and peace.

In Christ Alone

I believe one cannot create one's own narrative or identity for themselves... it's to be found in Christ, and in Christ alone!

I also believe that the only foundation strong enough for our lives is JESUS CHRIST. Without

Him, you cannot FULFILL your destiny. Your identity in Christ is really all you have. Outside of that you have nothing, and you are nothing. It is only in Christ Jesus where we have a common destiny as mankind. Since He is the only Way to the plan of God for our lives.

Jesus is the Key to success in life. If you are living your life without accepting the Lord, Jesus Christ you are living beneath your privileges. When you find Jesus, you find yourself — your true identity. And finding your true identity in Christ is the secret to a life of joy and love. The more you agree with God about your identity in Christ, the more your behavior will begin to reflect your GOD given identity.

GOD WANTS TO BLESS YOU! He wants to encounter you, and enable you to change your world! He wants to give you a new identity so that you may bring Glory to Him. The only thing is that, God can't bless the person that you pretend to be. He can only bless who you really are, the person He created you to be.

God wants to give you a new identity through Christ Jesus and make you a blessing. He wants to change your name (identity) like He changed:

⇨ **Abram**'s (high father) name to **Abraham** (father of many). *Read Genesis 17:5*

⇨ **Sarai** (my princess) to **Sarah** (mother of nations). *Read Genesis 17:15*

⇨ **Jacob** (supplanter) to **Israel** (he who has the power of God) *Read Genesis 32:28*

⇨ **Simon** (God has heard) to **Peter** (rock) *Read John 1:42*

And the list goes on!

Beloved, how you answer the question "Who Am I?" is a window into what you believe about God, and what you believe about God *determines* how you live your life. Embracing God's identity for you gives you the freedom to live out the amazing plan and purposes God has for you.

When you believe and receive God's identity for you then you begin the great journey of freedom to be all that God created you to be and to do all that God created you to do.

Security + Identity = Destiny.
Find your security in God's Love; Know who you are in Christ; and you will find your life purpose.

WHEN YOU DISCOVER WHO GOD IS, YOU DISCOVER WHO YOU ARE.

Chapter
TWO

Created On Purpose
For A Purpose

"The greatest tragedy in life is not death,
but a life without a purpose."

Myles Munroe

Have you ever *wondered* what your life purpose is? Do you believe God created you for a special purpose? Have you ever contemplated the fact that your destiny could change lives or even the world? What does God want you to do with your life? —Do not feel bad if your answer to these questions is no. You are not alone.

There are many millions of people who are trying to find purpose of life; some know exactly what their purpose is, and they are operating and walking in it. Some know what it is about but they are afraid to step into it. And others do not have a clue as to why they are on earth.

Each of us is born with a specific purpose, something God created us to do. Humans tend to leave things to chance, but not God. God is intentional in both His Words and deeds. Just like every creator have a purpose of its creation, God created us with a purpose and a design. We were imagined, planned, and lovingly created on purpose for a purpose.

Dr. Myles Munroe wrote in his book 'Purpose For Living'; "The potential of a thing is related to its source. This means wherever something comes from determines the potential it has. The degree or potency of that POTENTIAL can be measured by the demands made on it by the one who made it. Therefore, the potential or ability of a thing is determined by the purpose for which the creator, manufacture or maker made it."

In other words, every product is designed and engineered by the manufacture to FULFILL its purpose. You and I were designed to operate on purpose. God (our CREATOR) sees in us the potential to DOMINATE, rule and subdue the whole earth. Everything in the earth must be under our subjection, not mastering us! But of all the reasons God created us, the most important reason is to have a fellowship with Him. (See Genesis 1:26-28)

God created us for His glory. To glorify God is to acknowledge who God is (our Creator) and to praise and worship Him as such. The more we get to know our Creator and the more we love Him, the better we understand who we are and what our purpose is.

If you want to experience God's purpose for your life, experience God. Don't go looking for His will, look for Him. It is in the close, abiding intimacy with the Father (God) that you will not only discover, but you will also live out the destiny He has purposed for you.

Christian scholar and author, Sir. Os Guinness once said: "Answering the call of our Creator is "the ultimate why" for living, the highest source of purpose in human existence. Apart from such a calling, all hope of discovering a purpose will end in disappointment—Nothing short of God's call can ground and FULFILL the truest human desire for purpose."

Our purpose cannot be found except as we are connected to God because He is our Creator. If you want to know your purpose, you have to go where God is. It is only in God's presence that you can rediscover yourself and find your life purpose. Spending time in God's presence gives us perspective, planning and purpose.

Trust me, there is no place in the world like God's presence. It is the only place I have ever been where I have felt real love, real purpose and freedom. Every encounter with the Creator comes with a purpose. Every encounter with Him calls to a higher calling and a greater life. God knows why He made us, and if we will spend time with Him we will know our purpose.

Moses met God at a burning bush because he came to the mountain where God was hanging out. Now Moses didn't know he was going to meet GOD that day, but he was in God's presence. As I talk about it in the next chapter, Moses understood the power and purpose of God's presence in his life. He knew that it was God's presence that people would see and feel on him that would distinguish him.

God knows where He wants you, what He is calling you to do, when He wants you to do it, and how He wants it done. Therefore, if you want to find your purpose (calling), look for God. When you find God, His calling will find you. God's calling for your life, then, will be experienced out of your relationship with Him.

If there is no relationship, you will not come to know what your purpose (calling) is all about. If you never have time to go before the face of God, you won't find your purpose. If you never have time to spend in God's Word, you won't find His plan for your life. Today, I encourage you to press into God's presence until He moves you. When you do that you will experience the goodness of God and find your destiny to fulfill His purpose in your life.

God Was Intentional About You!

God had a wonderful purpose in mind when He began to reveal His artistry and wisdom in the creation of the universe.

In Ephesians 1:8-10 (NASB), the Apostle Paul gives us a rare insight into God's wonderful plan, not only for humanity but for all creation. He said, "In all wisdom and insight He made known to us the mystery of His will, according to His kind intention which He purposed in Him with a view to an administration suitable to the fullness of the times (eras), that is, the summing up of all things in Christ, things in the heavens and things on the earth."

It is exciting to know that God has a plan and purpose for everyone and everything, including the past, present and future!... Like my Mum says "Every day, every hour, and every minute has a purpose." God is the God of purpose and He has a plan for you. So before you question your circumstances, always remind yourself that everyone in your life has a purpose and everything happens for a reason.

When the odds are against you, remember God is for you. And that He has a purpose for your pain, a reason for your struggles, and a reward for your faithfulness.

He is taking you great places!

In Ephesians 2:10, the Bible says,

"…we are God's workmanship, created in Christ Jesus to do good works, which God prepared in advance for us to do."

Now, stop right there. Think about that. I mean really embrace it. God has a plan, and you are a part of it. Isn't it amazing! Not only that you are a part of God's plan, but you are also God's workmanship, recreated in Christ Jesus; to do exploits (good works) that God predestined for you.

Friend, your life is not a mistake. You are not optional. You are essential! You were in the plan of God when your daddy met your mommy! Remember what God said in Jeremiah 1:5, "Before I formed you in the womb I knew you, before you were born I set you apart." We are indeed God's workmanship.

The truth of Ephesians 2:10 dispels every insinuation of failure—it counters every lie and accusation that whispers; "Your life doesn't count. You don't have significance, your life is meaningless."

Friend, your life counts! You matter to God! Never let the devil trick you out of your promise. You are not here by accident. You were not born just because your parent decided to have children. You are not on the earth simply to

30

exist from day to day. Destiny is what God settled *concerning* you before He started forming you! You were in the thought of God from the beginning of the foundation of the world. God committed to choose you before you knew how to choose yourself. You are His child! You are deeply loved and are designed for a purpose.

Your purpose is as unique as God is Creative. You have significance because you belong to God. He gave you an identity and a purpose before you ever wondered why He created you. So quit listening to the lies and accusations of the enemy whose mission is *to kill, steal, and destroy.*

Instead, position your ears to hear God's plan. Invite Him to help you discover the distinct way you can best honor Him with your life.

Remember, it is in God's presence alone that 100% fulfillment is found! When you spend time in God's presence, in fellowship with the Holy Spirit, God's greater purpose flows through you; this is where your gifts, talents (skills), passion, experience and personality merge together into either the revealing of, or carrying out of… your destiny.

IF YOU CANNOT TRACE
GOD'S PURPOSE FOR YOUR LIFE…
YOU CAN NEVER LIVE A FULFILLED LIFE.

Fulfilling Your Purpose Brings Fulfillment ...

Everything in the world was created to solve a problem and fulfill a purpose; a toaster is created for a very specific PURPOSE, which is to toast bread. When a toaster toasts bread, it fulfills its creative purpose.

A car is created to transport human beings from one place to another. When a car transports people to where they want to go, it has fulfilled its creative purpose. And a guitar is created to provide its player and audience with the joys of music. Once the guitar is played to generate the sounds of music, it has fulfilled its purpose.

Now, in the same fashion, human beings were created to *worship, glorify,* and *enjoy* God! When we make worshiping, glorifying, and enjoying God the central purpose of our existence, we experience the joy of fulfillment.

Your GREATEST fulfillment will come from accepting and occupying God's unique place for you to the best of your ability. If you accept God's purpose for your life — your life will have fulfillment beyond measure. I have discovered that nothing brings fulfillment like doing the will of God. If you are looking for fulfillment outside of God's will, you won't find it.

Many people make the mistake of anticipating that their husband or wife, or someone else, or even something else will fulfill them, when in reality only God can meet our needs. No person is capable of bringing completion to another; humans cannot possibly fill this God-sized void within us. If we feel unfulfilled, it is because we have not fully grasped our ultimate purpose for living—to know and please God.

You need to UNDERSTAND that when God created you, He deposited in you every thing that you need in order to fulfill your purpose. God wants you to be fruitful, to multiply, to subdue, to live a fulfilled life. In fact, He has already equipped you with everything you need to live fulfilled and happy all the days of your life. It's time for you to stop living a life of activity and live a life of purpose!

Life is beautiful when you are walking in your purpose. Step into your purpose now! When you move, God will cause all that is required for the fulfillment of your destiny to converge toward you.

We can all agree that no one enjoys putting a puzzle together only to discover in the end that one piece is missing... You and I are an imperative and priceless piece of God's puzzle. Let's hone in on what we were created to conquer so that we can complete the beautiful picture God has laid out for us.

I encourage you to meditate on the things of

God. Meditate daily on His Word by reading the Bible—which is your truth. Let your relationship with God and the Holy Spirit be greater than your Spiritual gifts, talents, and abilities.

Ask God how to use those things to serve others and to perform the divine works set aside that only you can complete. Believe with all of your heart that you will do what you were created to do in Jesus name!

When you encounter God, He will lead you to your purpose… and your life will never be the same.

YOUR LIFE IS NOT A MISTAKE.

There is something phenomenal you were born to accomplish.

What Is In Your Hand?

*"God asks questions for our good, for our growth,
for our development and transformation."*

George Snyman

That question, "What is in your hand?" is one of the most important questions in life. We all have something great in our hands that God wants to use for His glory.

What is the thing God has place in your hands that you have abandon? What are the talents, gifts, and abilities that you are too afraid or unwilling to use for God? Do you believe that what you have in your hand is what God blesses and prosper you with?

In this chapter, I want you to understand this one thing before everything else; God can use the SIMPLE things you hold in your hands to touch the lives of others and bring glory to His name. Let me share a story from the Bible that I hope will encourage your heart, because I want you to know that If you only appreciate what you have in your hand, God will use it in His master plan.

We all know the story of the burning bush and Moses excuses before God (See Exodus 3). It was just an ordinary day in the life of a farm worker. When he got out of bed that morning, the day was of no special significance. As a shepherd, Moses job was to look after a flock of sheep that belonged to his father-in-law, and to find some grass for them to eat.

That particular day, Moses decided to lead the sheep to an area that was known as a wasteland; that is what the name of the place means. It was called "Horeb". So, there under a benign sun, the very image of freedom, contentment and peace, the shepherd leads his flock to find pasture along the lower mountain slopes.

But then all of a sudden his familiar routine was interrupted when he saw a bush that was on fire. In itself, this was not an unusual sight. However, what was strange was that although the bush was *blazing*, it was not being consumed. This aroused his curiosity.

I imagine Moses saying to himself, "What's going on here? I can't believe this! Why doesn't the bush burn up?" He decided to go toward this bush to see this strange sight. When he got there, the Bible says that God called for him from within the bush, and Moses answered, "Here I am". Now you must understand, that is the step that so many of us are missing. God calls for us to invite us into His purpose, but because we are so astray from His voice we do not answer.

God told Moses that He had seen the Egyptians oppression of the Israelites, and that Moses had been chosen to deliver them out of the hand of the Egyptians. Moses did not feel capable of the task... which he immediately tried to turn down. He was like "Oh God, look at me! Who am I to do this? I'm just a shepherd, how can I possibly do that? I don't even know what to say! They will not believe me... please God, You can send someone else."

Moses was not excited about this mission because he was comparing the challenge that lay ahead to his life up to that point. He gave God a list of excuses why he wasn't qualified to lead. He doubted himself. He didn't feel equipped. He was even SELF-CONSCIOUS because he had a stuttering problem.

Do you have similar excuses as Moses? Do you ever feel inadequate for what you are called to do? Or are you having trouble trusting that God is capable of equipping you for the work to which He has called you?... Is there anything holding you back from accepting God's call to serve Him?

Friend, God may assign you a demanding task, but I want you to realize that it is not about you — it is about who is with you! So stop giving God excuses and start giving Him obedience. God won't ask you to do anything He didn't equip you to do. He is greater than your excuses!

In the next few moments, God showed Moses that it didn't matter what equipment he thought he needed. The Bible says, God asked Moses, "What is that in your hand?" "A staff," Moses replied. God then told Moses to throw the staff on the ground, and when he did, it became a serpent. Then God said, "Take it by the tail," and it became a staff again. (See Exodus 4)

God knew what Moses had in his hand. God was not asking for information. God was asking for INSTRUCTION. God was asking Moses to carefully consider the thing he held in his hand. It was God's way of getting Moses to see that even the most ordinary things in our lives can become extraordinary when used in His service. God was telling Moses that He was going to use what was in his hand to take Egypt and shake it!

Can you IMAGINE what must have gone through Moses mind in that moment? After all, a staff is nothing more than a glorified stick! How was it going to make an impact in Pharaoh's court? There is nothing extraordinary about a staff. But understand this: "*the common becomes mighty when God anoints it.*" (Lisa Bevere)

The God that we serve has no difficulty at all creating something out of nothing. He took that stick, that weak, powerless, dead, dry stick and used it in a mighty way—it became one of the greatest SUPERNATURAL weapons in human history. God used what was in Moses hand to bring and remove the ten plagues and to open the waters of the Red Sea. The Bible says,

> *"God has given each of us the ability*
> *to do certain things well."*

Romans 12:6 (NLT)

WHAT IS IN YOUR HAND? Or let me put in another way, what kind of influence, power, gift, talent, or ability do you possess that God can enhance and multiply in you for the extension of His kingdom?

Like Moses we all have "a staff" in our hands. Something we can use to accomplish our part in God's work here on earth as we serve one another. This could be money, influence, gifts, talents, abilities, or possessions. It can be that little thing you constantly overlook—that one that you regard as nothing. God wants to use it! He wants to use that simple "staff" in your hand to show His POWER and AUTHORITY working through you! It is usually the insignificant thing everyone despises in you that God usually use to show His glory.

Now my question is, are you willing to let go (surrender) so that God can do a new thing in you? If Moses had held on to the staff he would have *remained* a shepherd. He would have spent the rest of his life counting sheep. Here is the bottom line: if you hold on to whatever is in your hand you will never *experience* the miracles God wants to perform!

Lay It Down And It Will Come Alive

Just like God showed Moses that He could work through whatever was in his hands as long as it was surrendered to Him. God is asking if you are willing to lay down your dead things so He can make them come to life. He is telling you today to lay it all down!

Lay down your influence and recognition. Lay down your plans and ambitions. Lay down your vision and your dreams. Lay down your gifts and talents. Lay down your position and title. Lay down your abilities and capacity. Lay down your past and your hurts. Lay down your uncertainties and your worry. Lay down your resources and possessions. Lay down your fear and insecurities. Just lay it all down!

The Lord said, "It may look like a mere stick (nothing), but if it needs to be a key to open a door, I will turn it into a key. If it needs to be a shield to protect you, I will turn it into a shield. If it needs to be healing to restore you, I will turn it into that. Just lay down whatever you have in your hand so I can use the ORDINARY to do something extraordinary in your life."

When God called me to full-time ministry. I was excited. But I was also scared. I have learned that whenever God calls us to take a leap of faith, fear is in the neighborhood yelling "don't jump" at the top of its voice! It was an agonizing decision for me.

I remember asking myself; "How will I pay my bills if I don't have a job? How will I feed and clothe myself and my family without the security of a paycheck? Where will I live when I get evicted or the bank forecloses on my house?" My faith was under major pressure because of my unbelief. Friends told me I was committing a grave mistake. But I felt like God was calling me to throw down my staff and embrace His calling without no back up plan!

I struggled with this for a year, until I realized that the One who has called me is faithful to WATCH OVER and PERFORM His Word! (See Jeremiah 1:12) It's a beautiful thing when you can embrace the will of God despite trembling heart, because you know how faithful the One who has called you is!

Beloved, don't be afraid of the unknown, God got you! He will never tell you to do something and not provide for you. GOD IS THE GREAT PROVIDER! Just lay it all down before Him and trust in His perfect plan! The faithful see the invisible, believe the incredible and then receive the impossible.

In order for Moses to see his STAFF as something that now had power, he had to do something. He had to lay it down! You can't receive what God has for you until you release what you have been holding onto.

I am trying to get you to understand that everything you hold in your hand is either a burden or a blessing depending upon what you do with it. When you hold on to it… it is a problem. When you yield it up to the Lord, He is able to release its potential for blessing in your life.

As far as God is concerned, what you have is enough! He can use the little you have and turn it into something bigger. What you think is a failure, God can use to MOVE you into your destiny. We serve a more than enough God! A running over God… who has a way of making miracles out of mistakes. He is the only One who can use disorder to create a new order in your life.

God wants to give you something new, but you have to be *willing* to let go of what you have. As the old folks said, "You can't fill a cup that is already full." God can't give you something new if you are still clenching onto old things. You have to release what you have so you can receive what God has for you.

Today, the Lord is ready and willing to anoint what is in your hands... Are you willing to let Him? If only you will take what you have and give it to God. He will make it come alive!

Little is much when God is in it.

DON'T BE AFRAID OF THE UNKNOWN, GOD GOT YOU!

Chapter
FOUR

Whatever You Need You Already Have

"When you are faithful with what you have in your hand, then God can bless it and multiply it."

Victoria Osteen

One of the GREATEST problems we have as believers is we have a tendency to underestimate what we have and overestimate what we don't have. So often we feel we need extraordinary abilities to do God's work. The truth is, we all already possess whatever we need to live a life that pleases God—and to do His work.

In second Peter 1:3, the Bible says, "We have everything we need to live a life that pleases God. It was all given to us by God's own power, when we learned that he had invited us to share in his wonderful goodness." (CEV). God created us with a unique blend of talents and passions to impact the world and make a difference in other people's lives, yet so many fail to embrace them.

Many are still hoping God will give them gifts and talents. But the Bible tells us that God has already given us everything we need to live a life that pleases Him. The only thing we lack is revelation of what we already have! We cannot ask God for anything more than what He has already given us;

• **Life**	• **Wisdom**
• **Gifts**	• **Knowledge**
• **Talents**	• **Salvation**
• **Courage**	• **Faith**
• **Comfort**	• **Peace**
• **Love**	• **Joy**
• **Healing**	• **Strength**
• **Victory**	• **Freedom**
• **Success**	• **Wealth**
• **Prosperity**	• **Power**
• **Authority**	• **Patience**
• **Favor**	• **Mercy**

And many more…

We also have the most important person on earth with us everyday; the HOLY SPIRIT. He is our number one Helper in fulfilling our destiny. He is the Spirit of the Lord. He is fully God. He is eternal, omniscient, and omnipresent. He is also the Chief Executive of the divine program on earth. He is the One in charge of the affairs of the Kingdom of God on earth today.

The Holy Spirit is behind every exploit in the Kingdom of God. If you need wisdom and understanding, counsel and strength, knowledge and fear of the Lord, then He is the right person to connect with! (See Isaiah 11:2)

Above all these great gifts, the GREATEST gift we have ever received is our Lord and Savior **JESUS CHRIST**. The giver of Life. The Savior of the world. Creator of the universe. The Alpha and Omega. The Beginning and the End. The First and the Last. The Wisdom and the Word of God. The Chief Cornerstone. The King of kings and Lord of lords. The Bread of Life. The Light in our darkness. The Son of the Living God. He is the Way, the Truth, and the Life.

Before there was a where or a when or this or that, before there was anybody there to write a song or a book about Him… **HE WAS GOD**! Our human finite vocabulary does not contain enough words to describe an infinite God that He Is! Our Lord is not restricted by space and time. He exists beyond our universe and beyond our limitations. With Him on your side and the strength of the Holy Spirit, you can do whatever you need to do!

I challenge you not to ask God for more. Instead, thank Him for what you already have then access it! Use what is in your hand and God will use what is in your heart to do things beyond your wildest dreams!

Beloved, God has a unique role for you to play in His plan for this generation. This is your ministry (purpose), and God has gifted you for this assignment; to perform a function within the body of Christ with Supernatural joy, energy, and effectiveness. He has placed you here on earth as a unique person with a unique mission aimed at ESTABLISHING and EXTENDING His Kingdom on earth as it is in Heaven.

Do you know that, there are no insignificant parts to God's family? We are all a part of the body of Christ, and all of the parts matter! Yes, you are significant! God has equipped you for your purpose and destiny... and everything in between! He has empowered you, and enabled you to handle everything that comes your way! So you need to be comfortable in the gifting the Lord has given you... and step into your place of power!

Now tell me, what do you already have in your possession that God can use to make you a BLESSING to others and ANSWER your needs; Writing? Teaching? Encouraging? Money? Life experiences? Speaking ability? Artistic ability?

Whatever your gifts, talents, or abilities are, do you trust God enough to open your hand and give it to Him? God never directs our attention to what we don't have, but to what we do have even though it seems small. Moses had a simple shepherd's staff. And God used it to do miracles when Moses obeyed Him. I firmly believe that what God is going to use to bless you in this season of your life is already in your possession. What you are looking for, you already have!

Don't Underestimate What You Have

One of the amazing thing about God is that, when He wants to solve a big problem He likes to use what is in our hands, even if it seems like it is nothing or inconsequential. A rod in Moses hands parted the Red Sea. A slingshot and one stone in David's hands killed a giant. Nails in Jesus hands produced salvation for the world. All of these men IMPACTED the history of the world.

It is time to recognize that the Lord will never give you a dream without the proper resources to bring that dream to pass. Like L. Bevere said, "When God is with you, it really doesn't matter what is in your hand... only that you use it."

It is time to stop sitting on your hands and waiting for time and chance to happen unto you. You already possess everything that you need to reach your destiny. God has already empowered you to prosper. Start with what you have!

Wherever you are, whatever you are doing... Step out in faith and begin to maximize what has been placed in your hands and watch that dream turn into reality. Quit looking at what you don't have. God is saying, "I can become what you need! It doesn't matter the size of your resources, it matters the size of your Faith! Trust Me, I can use your little if only you have FAITH! There is nothing too little or too small or too big for Me to handle."

Beloved, do not despise the little you have right now; what you see as just ordinary, God can make it extraordinary. He will give you the grace and the resources needed to make it work on your behalf. In fact, He has already placed on your path, the right people and resources to get the job done. So don't wait until circumstances are ideal to do your best. Be FAITHFUL with what is in your hand today, and God will bless it tomorrow.

Sampson had a donkey jawbone to slay a thousand men. Ruth had grain gleaned from the field. The unnamed boy had his five loaves and two fishes. The woman had an alabaster jar filled with oil to anoint Jesus. Don't limit what God can do with your life. Whatever is in your hand, He can do something extraordinary with it!

God is not moved by excuses. God is moved by faith.

DO NOT DESPISE THE LITTLE YOU HAVE...

WHAT YOU SEE AS JUST ORDINARY, THE LORD CAN MAKE IT EXTRAORDINARY.

Chapter
FIVE

From Pain
To Purpose

*"Every crisis you go through is an opportunity
for a new beginning in your life."*

Jerry Bonsu

In all of our lives, there are *moments* of darkness
and pain, and sometimes that pain seems too
great to overcome. I know that feeling well. But
what I have learned is that there is a way to take
that pain and use it to DISCOVER your true
purpose on this earth. There is a way to turn
pain into purpose.

The fact is that pain is a part of life. To never
have any pain in your life is to be inhuman. If
God didn't spare Jesus, His only Son from pain;
what makes you think He will spare you? Pain
has a purpose in every area of our lives. It is part
of the birthing process. It is a necessary part of
the *process* to be everything God called you to be.

Pain is an incredibly effective tool to achieve God's purposes in our lives: transforming us into the image of Christ Jesus, tearing down strongholds that keep us from being all that God made us to be, restoring what was lost in the Fall.

Since God has no magic wand and no Easy button (that's only for Staples commercials), He has to use other means to ACCOMPLISH the considerable task of changing people who are far more broken and messy and less than we were created to be, into the people He intended us to be from the beginning.

As you have heard before: "There's no GREATNESS without some kind of painful experience." When you are a child of destiny, you have to understand that God has a purpose for your pain! God never allows pain without a purpose in the lives of His children. In fact God has a purpose in every pain He allows in our lives. He has a purpose behind every problem that we encounter. God never wastes pain. He always uses it to accomplish His purpose… and causes it to work together for our ultimate good.

What you need to understand is that, God uses pain to grow us. He uses it to develop the qualities that are necessary for us. Every obstacle we experience is an opportunity for soul growth, self-empowerment and personal advancement. Any trail a believer faces can ultimately bring glory to God because God can bring good out of any bad situation.

Pain often reveals God's purpose for us. The problem is we often don't understand it. We don't realize what the good is. We don't see any PURPOSE in it and if pain doesn't have any purpose, it is very difficult to handle.

Pain is power and should be used to fuel our purpose, increase wisdom and awareness... and provoke growth and maturity. Unfortunately, most of us use it as a crutch to hurt others, over eat, use drugs and alcohol, blame others, and not be accountable, among other things, and that is okay... (*Ummm? I don't think so!*) Wouldn't you prefer to create power and purpose from your pain?

The world has taught us many myths about pain that just isn't true. Some of them are harmless, but one very destructive myth is this: "If you ignore your pain it will go away." The truth is God doesn't want us to ignore our pain. He wants us to discover the cause so we can find real relief.

Pain is like a warning light... it shows us that there is something wrong with the way we are living, and that we need to change it. As it is not wise to ignore a warning light—you can't ignore your pain. You must recognize it as God's denial buster and open YOURSELF up to the hope and power He offers.

A writer once said, "Our deepest life message often comes out of our deepest pain. We grow deeper and far greater in the valleys rather than on the mountaintops. That is just the way we are made." Pain is the high cost of *growth*. Whenever God means to make a man GREAT. He always breaks him in pieces first!

I wrote a book called "*God Is Up To Something Great*" about how God can turn any mess into a message, any test into a testimony, any trial into a triumph, and any victim into a victor… based on the story of Joseph in the Bible. The first chapter of his life is like a horror story; for everything that could go wrong did go wrong.

For years, he was neglected and he was rejected… he was sold into slavery by his brothers and falsely accused of rape and was thrown into prison. And the worst part of the story is that he was forgotten in prison. Joseph's whole life is just one PAINFUL experience after another. (See Genesis 37 to 50) But if you read the end of the story, you realize God was preparing him and through those circumstances he ended up being second in command in Egypt and saved not only Egypt, but he also saved Israel.

At the end of his life Joseph says, "You intended to harm me, but God intended it for good to accomplish what is now being done, the saving of many lives." (Genesis 50:20)

All along in Joseph's life, God was goading, guiding, gauging, guarding and growing joseph for greatness. Little did Joseph know the darkest day of his life paved the path of DESTINY... God used his suffering (*pain*) and his subsequent circumstances to accomplish His own sovereign purpose!

Beloved, unless you see the big picture of what God is doing through the difficulties of life, the suffering, the pain, the injustices of life, you will miss the profound and foundational truth that God is using all of it for your ultimate good and His glory. The Lord often uses our deepest pain as the launching pad of our greatest calling.

Like Joseph, you may not always understand what is happening to you, but the Lord is always in control. He is using the pain to prepare you for GREATNESS. You have to be willing to go through the process to get connected to God's true purpose.

Do you know that getting to the place where God ultimately wants you is also up to you to surrender to His will? Total surrender to God is the surest way to achieve your potential. Joseph chose to allow God to bring purpose from his pain. He did not let his hardships make him bitter; he chose to trust God and become better.

People may hurt you, plans may fail you, but God will turn it into good if you choose to remain faithful. It is not about how others treat you; it is about how you respond. Let your pain have purpose. Don't let it dictate your future! Pain may endure through the night, but joy comes in the morning! (See Psalm 30:5)

Maintaining a joyful spirit, having a prayerful mind and a thankful attitude is God's will for all believers. When trouble comes, do you grumble, complain, and blame God, or do you see your pain and problems as opportunities to honor God? Be thankful in all circumstances and in all things. Trust God in the process. And believe that out of all the pain something beautiful will prevail. God is up to something great!

The Power of Your Testimony!

Do you know that there is something valuable about you that God wants to use for the up-building of His Kingdom? God wants to use your testimony! Yes! Your Story! Because your story is the key that can unlock someone else's prison.

I believe that God can use the testimony of our past to give someone else a future. He can use our life EXPERIENCES to draw others to Him. That is why you should never be ashamed of your story. No matter how you may feel about it, there is someone somewhere who needs to hear how you overcome!

Whenever I am going through trials I always remind myself that this is just yet another way I can one day help others who will one day walk through that same trial. It will be just one more opportunity for me to use my own testimony to help unlock someone else's prison.

Whatever you went through was necessary! It was part of God's divine plan. What you have experience was not just for you! You went through it for somebody else's victory. You were going through to make someone else's life better than it is. That is why you had to survive your storm.

The enemy did not think you would still be STANDING in praise after all you have come through. But God positioned you to SURVIVE because He knew you would be the tool to help bring deliverance in someone else's life. In fact, He wants to redeem your story and use it for something greater.

God has a way of turning our broken pieces into a MASTERPIECE! So don't worry! Your purpose is greater than your pain. No matter how good or bad your story is, don't keep it inside. It's not for you to hide; it's for you to share!

The Lord wishes to use your story to save others. When God moves in your life, you can't afford to not share your testimony! Your story can have a powerful impact on someone else's life, even if it is just a little part of that story! It will be one more way you can use to glorify God. (See 1 Chronicles 16:8).

Before we close this chapter, I want you to remember that your purpose is birthed through your pain and your passion. The very thing you are most ashamed of in your life and resent the most could become your greatest ministry in helping other people.

Like Bishop TD Jakes said, "God's way of escape may come through the very thing that you dislike the most about yourself! There is something in you that God wants to use... you are somebody's cure!" God is not punishing you—He is preparing you! Get ready! He is about to use your pain to catapult you into your purpose (calling)!

It is my prayer that God gives you strength in your struggle, peace in your pain, and victory in your valley. May He open the door of your heart and use whatever darkness, shame and pain hidden in there for His glory in the Mighty name of Jesus! Amen!

You survived for a reason!

THERE IS NO
GREATNESS
WITHOUT SOME
KIND OF PAINFUL
EXPERIENCE.
TRUST GOD
IN THE
PROCESS.

Destined For Greatness

"You are called to succeed, break ground, and make a difference."

Jerry Bonsu

I believe that we are all destined for greatness. When God created us, He DESIGNED us for accomplishment, engineered us for success, and endowed each of us with the seeds of greatness. We were fashioned in the image of God, and suited for a great purpose. Greatness is the birthright and assignment of every child of God.

God wants us to be great at whatever He has called us to do. If you are a teacher, God wants you to be a great teacher. If you are a leader, He wants you to be a great leader… to use your influence for Him and His glory. If you are a sports person He wants you to be great at it. Whatever is your calling or purpose, God wants you to be outstanding.

We are all called to greatness. And it is our portion and expected end. Unfortunately, there are some among us who are unhappy with their lives because they have wanted to achieve a measure of greatness in this life but now feel they have failed in some fundamental way. We have concern for those who have worked hard and who have lived righteously but think because they haven't achieved in the world or in the Church what others have achieved—they have failed. Perhaps we should consider the things that make a person great.

We live in a world that seems to worship its own kind of GREATNESS. It is true that the world's heroes don't last very long in the public mind, but nevertheless, there is never a lack of champions and great achievers. We hear almost daily of athletes breaking records; scientists inventing marvelous new devices, machines, and processes; and doctors saving lives in new ways.

We are CONSTANTLY being exposed to exceptionally gifted musicians and entertainers, also to the work of unusually talented artists, architects, and builders. Magazines, billboards, and television commercials bombard us with pictures of individuals with perfect teeth and flawless features, wearing stylish clothes and doing whatever it is that successful people do.

Because we are being constantly exposed to the world's definition of GREATNESS, it is understandable that we might frequently find ourselves making comparisons between who we are and what others are, or seem to be, and also between what we have and what others have.

Although it is true that sometimes making comparisons can be beneficial and may motivate us to accomplish much good and improve our lives, yet we often allow unfair and improper comparisons to destroy our happiness when they cause us to feel unfulfilled or inadequate or UNSUCCESSFUL... Sometimes, because of these feelings, we are led into error, and we dwell on our failures while ignoring aspects of our lives that may contain elements of true greatness!

Friend, don't allow comparison to steal your joy! Another person's greatness does not mean the absence of your own. Remember, you are destined for greatness, and nothing can change that! Don't let the world measure your greatness, when the world has yet to even realize it's own potential.

A.W. Tozer was right when he said, "Our society has fallen into the error of assuming that greatness and fame are synonymous." People of nowadays mistake fame and greatness. But I don't think you have to be famous to attain greatness. Fame is about what you get; greatness is about what you give.

The world defines GREATNESS in terms of power, possessions, prestige, and position. Jesus, however, *measured* greatness in terms of service, not status. (See Mark 10:43) Greatness for the Kingdom begins when you align yourself with God's agenda for the benefit of others. Like Pastor Rick Warren said, "Greatness in God's book (the Bible) is not measured by how many *people* serve you, but by how many people you serve."

True greatness isn't the kind that appears in bold letters on your favorite website. No! It's about knowing your purpose in life and sowing into the lives of others. It is the quality that radiates from the inside out. It is who you are when you are honoring your values and living a life of purpose. TRUE GREATNESS is not how bright you shine, but how bright you make others shine.

Greatness is your destiny. It is God's idea for your life. That is why God refuse to define the greatness of your life in money or wealth, positions or titles, family or friends, promotions or raises, fame or fortune, accomplishments or recognition. Your greatness is not what you have or what you have achieved… it is what you give!

Riches may make you FAMOUS, but true greatness comes from serving others. If you aspire to be great, give yourself to the small, mundane, easily over-looked needs around you.

Serve your generation with your gifts, talents, and abilities. Be the type of person that adds value to lives no matter where you go. Be the kind of person who makes others feel special. Be a blessing and be blessed!

In the words of Carlos Santana, "There is no greater reward than working from your heart and making a difference in the world!" Indeed, there is no greater reward (on earth) than knowing that, in some small way, you have helped a follow human.

As we read earlier, we are called to greatness and destined for glory. Don't wait for the world to recognize your greatness. Live it! Believe it! And let the world catch up with you!

Greatness Takes Sacrifice

Everyone is worthy of GREATNESS, but not everyone is willing to sacrifice and do what it takes to be great. Sir Winston S. Churchill once said "The price of greatness is responsibility." So many people want to be great, but most of them are not willing to pay the price for it.

The potential for a life of greatness lies within each of us, but we must be committed to some specific principles. Greatness is a choice... It is not a function of circumstance. It is a matter of conscious choice and discipline. You can't be great without discipline. A PREREQUISITE for greatness is self discipline. Greatness requires physical, mental, spiritual *and* emotional control. The road to achieve greatness can be a very hilly road. Why? Because nothing in life comes easy. When you sign up for greatness, pain is built into the contract. greatness requires sacrifices, obstacles and roadblocks… and as we all know, there is no sacrifice without pain.

There is a price to pay for greatness. Although it is true that God has destined us for greatness, it comes at a cost. Jesus already paid the price to make us great, but we also must pay some of the price in order to attain the greatness that our God has destined for us. The Scriptures provide information on some of the things our Lord Jesus (the Greatest of all time) went through in order to pay the price for our greatness.

Isaiah 53:1-12 details the suffering of our God. In verses 3-7, we read: "He was despised and rejected by mankind, a man of suffering, and familiar with pain. Like one from whom people hide their faces he was despised, and we held him in low esteem. Surely he took up our pain and bore our suffering, yet we considered him punished by God, stricken by him, and afflicted. But he was pierced for our transgressions, he was crushed for our iniquities; the punishment that brought us peace was on him, and by his wounds we are healed. We all, like sheep, have gone astray, each of us has turned to our own way; and the Lord has laid on him the iniquity of us all. He was oppressed and afflicted, yet he did not open his mouth; he was led like a lamb to the SLAUGHTER, and as a SHEEP before its shearers is silent, so he did not open his mouth."

Apart from the price that Jesus paid,
we also must be ready to pay the price in
other to achieve greatness.

Again the Scripture contains examples of people who paid the price of greatness. Do you remember Joseph? The guy who was sold into slavery by his brothers, and was falsely accused of rape and was thrown into prison. We read in the Scripture that the Lord was with Joseph and He made everything Joseph did to prosper— because Joseph was willing to pay the price of greatness. The Bible says, God turned the evil his brothers planned for him into his good… and he became great in spite of their evil plans.

Friend, the price of greatness never goes on sale. Are you willing to pay the full price? As I said earlier, greatness is built on the virtue of sacrifice. You have to be willing to pay the price of greatness in order to enjoy the prize.

It is said; if it doesn't challenge you, it won't change you. Don't let your pain hold you back from greatness. Let the pain be a spring- board to your next level of greatness. Don't let fear, doubt, unbelief keep you from moving forward! Be bold and embrace the greatness within you and move forward with confidence. The same God that was with Joseph is still our God and He is ready to help us if we depend on Him.

Understand this, the role of God in walking towards greatness cannot be put behind by anybody. For no success comes outside God. You have a seeds of greatness inside of you. Your identity is in Christ (the Greatest of all time). Therefore, true Greatness is in your DNA. You are unstoppable! You are stronger, smarter, and more resilient than you think. You are capable of achieving far more than you believe. You were meant for greatness—like our Lord Jesus Christ.

Today, believe that God is the author of your story. He wrote it from the beginning to the end. The plans He has in store for you will happen. Nothing can stop what God has placed within you. Not even the devil!

Beloved, never underestimate the power and authority that has been given to you by God through Christ Jesus to overcoming, conquering, and dominating fears, obstacles, or anything that gets in your way! BREAK OUT of the limited mindset! You have greatness in you. Where you are is not where you are supposed to stay. It's time to stand in your greatness and shine!!!

Greatness is your destination.

YOU ARE
DESTINED FOR
GREATNESS,
AND NOTHING
CAN CHANGE
THAT!

Chapter
SEVEN

Birthing The Purpose

*"The birthing of your destiny and purpose
can only come through you."*

Jerry Bonsu

When we talk about birthing a purpose, the first thing we need to know is that birthing is a KINGDOM PRINCIPLE. It is a principle that originated from God. God always does things based on principle. When He wanted to make a change in the universe (earth), the first thing He did was get in a birthing position.

The Bible says, "And the earth was without form, and void; and darkness was upon the face of the deep. And the Spirit of God moved upon the face of the waters." (See Genesis 1 :2) The Hebrew word for "moved" means brooded or hovered, as when a mother bird broods over her eggs to bring forth life.

This indicates that after God's judgment God did something to bring forth LIFE. The situation was really WASTE and VOID, and there was darkness upon the depth of the water. Then the Spirit of God came in to brood, to hover, over the situation in order to produce life.

Following this, from Genesis 1:3 to the end of chapter two, there is a long record of how life was brought forth through the brooding of the Spirit. What I need you to recognize is that, all of us are carrying a vision (dream) that has been planted in us as a seed and we have been chosen to birth the vision.

We all have a seed of destiny that God has planted in our lives. Every single one of us has a seed hidden in the soil of our hearts. The seed is Supernatural abilities intended to be used to bring forth God's plan in the earth!

One day I was thinking of what God has placed in my heart to do for His Kingdom. I have a God-ordained desire to empower and equip YOUNG LEADERS to work from their community to reachout into the world to spread a Kingdom massage far and wide—and helping them to fulfill their highest calling and usher them into a Supernatural lifestyle of faith and abundant living.

I asked the Lord one time, "Father, how is this vision (dream) going to ever come into reality?" He said to me: "Son, you are going to have to bring it forth by **intimacy**, **pregnancy**, **travail**, and **birth**." Then He added, "I want you to win and boldly decide to birth that vision no matter what circumstances you may be facing."

That is when I discover that when God gives you a VISION or a DREAM, it is like becoming pregnant: He conceived in you the vision. He birthed something inside you. He planted the seed that will bring forth good fruit. In other words, you become pregnant with purpose and possibilities.

Every vision or purpose requires a birthing process. Just like a natural pregnancy, there is a gestation period; a time period when your vision is shaped, structured and developed. Once that vision reaches full maturity, there is a birthing process... and that is when the hardest work begins! But how we go from the **expecting** phase to the **birth** phase is what determines if our vision survives and thrives.

Understanding the process is key to having success and bringing your dream to fulfillment.

The birthing process will involve preparation and planning before labor and delivery take place. You will experience birthing pains. There will be adjustments and changes you will be required to make. There will be trials. You may feel like giving up when going from place to place. It may seem like forever. But in the midst of it all, DON'T GIVE UP! There is no birthing without some pain—it's a part of God's process.

Don't lose sight of purpose in the process of what God is working in you. Just hold on! God knows what He is doing. He will send those He has assigned to help you birth the vision that He has placed inside of you.

Conceiving Your Dream

A birth always begins with conception. If you can't conceive that God can and wants to do something amazing with your life, you will never take the first step toward a better life than what you have now.

To conceive, you must believe! Believing is the first part of conceiving your God-given dream. Jesus says, "It shall be done for you as you have believed." (See Matthew 8:13 AMP) Whatever the heart can conceive and believe, the mind can achieve.

Conceiving is a revelation and a powerful tool for breakthrough. To conceive and give birth to the miracles you need, you must first plant God's Word like a seed in your heart. Since the Holy Spirit is the Source of Conception… He has the capacity to conceive in you the mind of God. (See Matthew 1:20).

The truth is, before you birth the supernatural, you must first conceive by the Holy Spirit. He is the One who gives us the ability to see dreams, visions and things to come. He says, "I will pour out my Spirit on all people. Your sons and daughters will **prophesy**, your old men will dream **dreams**, your young men will see **visions**." (Joel 2 :28)

So friend, if you have perceived what you know God wants you to do and you believe it… it is important to carry it and guide it and not allow it to be aborted.

Get excited about it! Be happy! Just as a farmer knows his crops will grow, as a mother believes her baby will be great… know your dream, believe with all your heart… knowing that what God is about to do in your life, no EYE has seen, no EAR has heard, and no MIND has imagined. (See 1 Corinthians 2:9)

Seasons Of Preparation

Seasons of preparation are not only for young adults who are training for their future. Seasons of PREPARATION occur throughout our life, preceding new levels in our relationships, influence, contributions, ministry or career.

God has PURPOSE in everything, including the transitions necessary for our advancement, a time to make us ready for what is ahead. God has a wide variety of purposes for seasons of transition, but all are meant to prepare us for going higher in Him.

When you are in the season of preparation, you may begin to feel like it's taking longer than you thought it would, it's harder than you expected it would be, and it's costing more than you ever thought you would have to pay. That is the time when you need to choose to walk by faith, TRUSTING God even though you don't understand everything, so He can do the work that needs to be done in you.

God has something planned for you, and if you are not living in the fulfillment of His plan for you, then now is the season of preparation. Every purpose has season of preparation. So rest assured, you are not alone! We all go through times like this. The Bible tells us that even Jesus needed time to grow and increase in wisdom, stature and in years before He was ready to make a GLOBAL IMPACT through His three-year ministry (See Luke 2:52).

Ecclesiastes 5:3, says, "A dream comes with much business and painful effort..." (AMPC) In other words, you have to be willing to put forth the effort to do what God is showing you to do, and it isn't always easy. But when you are determined to trust God, believe in the dream He has put in your HEART and not give up, He will be faithful to give you everything you need to succeed.

PUSH!!!

You see, too many people give up living their dreams in the season of preparation, because they are living their fears, doubts, and anxieties. They abort their dreams before they reach full-term.

Pastor Joyce Meyer said, "God plants a seed (dream) in them and they become pregnant. But when they find out it will take effort, be costly and uncomfortable to complete their preparation for the birth, they decide it wasn't really GOD'S WILL after all and go and do something else."

I believe that many people in our generation are spiritually pregnant right now with dreams that God has placed within their belly—and yet have not been able to give birth to that dream. The problem that most of us face is not the promise (dream) or the provision for it… It is the process we endure to procure the promise. This PROCESS often threatens to abort the promise (dream) before it is brought to full fruition.

Friend, whatever SEASON you find yourself in right now, know that it is where you are supposed to be. Don't allow pain, fear, anxiety, doubt, insecurity, or naysayers to cause you to abort the vision that God has placed within you.

The most painful stage happens right before birth. This is known as "transition", and it can be excruciating. The doctor announces, "You are in transition" as if its good news! Then you are told not to push, but when you can't stand one more minute of pain, that is when the doctor says, PUSH! At that time, if you bear down and refuse give up, it isn't long before the baby is born.

In the birthing process for your dream, God tells you not to push in your own strength or wisdom, but to wait until it is time to push by His grace, strength and wisdom. Then, through a great deal of prayer, faith and determination, something miraculous happens. The very thing that caused you the most agony becomes the catalyst to bring your vision into existence. And that experience brings amazing joy!

John 16:21 tells us that,

"A woman giving birth to a child has pain because her time has come; but when her baby is born she forgets the anguish because of her JOY that a child is born into the world."

So hold on! Don't stop the process of birthing what God has placed down on the inside of you. God has designed a birthing time, a "delivery date" for your purpose and destiny to be made a reality in the Kingdom—and that time is NOW!

Don't take the treasure God placed within you

to the grave, stand and fight for it! Your God-given dreams are not religious options, but they are prophetic imperatives. The Lord says, "I am getting ready to birth something Great through you". Let the promise crown in this season. And watch the Lord turn your REVELATION into manifestation.

It's time to PUSH and birth your dreams into reality.

PUSH!

Benefits Of Knowing
Your Life Purpose

1. Knowing your life purpose allows you to define and lead a fulfilling life.

2. Knowing your life purpose will allow you to step away from activities and responsibilities that are not in alignment with that purpose... giving you more time for yourself.

3. Knowing your life purpose frees you from the need to compare yourself with others who have a totally different focus for their lives.

4. Knowing your life purpose gives you the courage to step out into something new when you recognize that you are especially equipped for that activity.

5. Knowing your life purpose validates and re-enforces the sense of peace and joy that comes from spending more time in areas that are congruent with your purpose.

6. Knowing your life purpose will allow you to better define those things that truly will make you happy.

7. Knowing your life purpose will allow you to easily recognize the walls your ladder may be leaning against which are the "wrong" walls.

8. Knowing your life purpose is a great time to take a fresh look at your spiritual beliefs.

9. Knowing your life purpose allows you to discover Who God Is... and who you really are.

10. Knowing your life purpose will allow you to redefine what success really means to you.

11. Knowing your life purpose allows you to relax and recognize that trusting God is the best thing you can do.

12. Knowing your life purpose will help chart the path toward making a difference in the world.

Romans 8:19 (CEB) says, "The whole creation waits BREATHLESS with anticipation for the revelation of God's sons and daughters." In other words, the world is waiting for our manifestation! God placed us on the earth at this time so that we can become the generation of people who shift the world for God! May the Lord help us to always represent the Kingdom of God… and bring change to this world!

Before you close this book, I want to remind you that difficult doesn't mean impossible, it simply means that you have to work hard and trust God's plan. When you BELIEVE in your greater purpose and have faith in the process to get there… there will be no suffering along the way only sacrifice.

The waiting, the meantime, the in-between, the delays and detours —It all serves a purpose. Just believe in yourself and stand upon God's promises. Enjoy the journey, make the most of every moment, and turn negatives into positives by learning from them.

God is building you up to give you access to things you have never imagined. This is your time to move forward with ZEAL of the Lord. Time to tap into your purpose!

Friend, God has granted you access to His purpose… all He is asking is that you trust Him, and He will supersede your expectations. Your purpose awaits. It's time for you to move! Move into God's presence! Move into His Word! When you step into God's promises, you will leap into your purpose!

It is my prayer that God help you to birth your purpose like never before. May He grant you the ability to do great works in Him. Since you are destined for greatness! May you begin to walk toward that destination! I pray you be great in your field, and outside of your field, and that God will grant you Supernatural understanding in your mind.

In this season of your life, may the Lord give you the *kind of mind* that you need to accomplish your purpose and that you will feel an urgency of purpose from the very depths of your soul in the Mighty name of Jesus! Amen!

BE A WORLD CHANGER TODAY!

EPILOGUE

It's been my honor to spend this journey with you and to share a bit of my experience on how to discover life true purpose and meaning. You have a legacy to fulfill and to leave behind.

My CHALLENGE to you here is to work on learning about *yourself* so that you can recognize your value. If you believe in yourself as much as God believes in you, then you will walk in a confidence that is even more of a threat to the enemy.

Your position is needed in the Kingdom. God is not through with you. He is just getting started with you! Your delight is connected to your desires and you have the power. You deserve to pursue your purpose, and when you are ready to walk into your purpose God will make a way, and He will make the crooked path straight for you.

God is more then able to do whatever He needs to do to get you to the place you need to be. Trust Him at His Word.

God bless you!
Jerry BONSU

BONUS MATERIAL

DEAR DREAMER: SESSION 1
An excerpt from amazon best seller book
"Dear Dreamer" by Jerry Bonsu

DEAR
DREAMER

JERRY BONSU

SESSION 1

Living the God-Sized Dream

Dear Dreamer
The fear of the LORD is the beginning of wisdom.

Dear Dreamer
What GOD originates, He orchestrates.

Dear Dreamer
If you can dream it, you can DO it.

Dear Dreamer
GOD expects you to cultivate, maintain and protect the gifts He has given you.

Dear Dreamer
Whenever GOD gives the VISION.... He also gives the PROVISION.

Dear Dreamer
Dream BIGGER than where you are right Now!

Dear Dreamer
GOD is glorified when you produce fruit.

Dear Dreamer
Don't let where you are make you forget where you are going. #Destiny

Dear Dreamer
Don't bring your dreams to the level of your resources. Keep on dreaming and believing... GOD will work the resources. #JehovahJireh

Dear Dreamer
Your DESTINY is greater than your distractions! #Focus

Dear Dreamer
Refuse to live your LIFE being controlled by the spirit of fear.

Dear Dreamer
Don't allow what you see to determine what you say! For we walk by FAITH, not by sight.

Dear Dreamer
Why focus on those in the opposite corner... If GOD be for you, who can be against you?

Dear Dreamer
The PROCESS always precedes the PROMISE. #AskJoseph

Dear Dreamer
Don't stop trying because you're afraid of failure... Be COURAGEOUS in the face of fear.

Dear Dreamer
Your dreams will cause you to step out on FAITH.

Dear Dreamer
You can be who GOD said you can be.

Dear Dreamer
SEEDS need to be dropped, pushed down, and buried before they rise — just like DREAMS. #BePartient

Dear Dreamer
Dreams are not achieved by magic or even by prayer alone… sacrifice comes before success. #DreamBIG… #WorkHard

Dear Dreamer
Never despise humble beginnings… Before JESUS wore a crown, He was a carpenter.

Dear Dreamer
May GOD give you the desire of your heart and make all YOUR plans succeed.

Dear Dreamer
If you can accomplish the VISION by yourself, then it's not from GOD. Because with GOD you need FAITH.
.
Dear Dreamer
GOD is touching someone to bless you. Even if people don't want Him to!

Dear Dreamer
GOD is using your circumstances to position

and prepare you to accomplish HIS vision for
your Life.

Dear Dreamer
If you've lost hope, remind yourself of the dream
GOD gave you. There is more to life than where
you are right now! #DreamAgain

Dear Dreamer
GOD knows WHEN to show you WHAT.
#TrustHim

Dear Dreamer
When you operate from a state of abundance
there is no room for hate or jealousy.

Dear Dreamer
GOD will not allow you to walk in obedience
and suffer embarrassment.

Dear Dreamer
When you know where GOD has brought you
from… you don't question where He is taking
you.

Dear Dreamer
Listen for GOD. Listen to GOD. And then do
what He says.

Dear Dreamer
NEVER let people PUSH you…. where GOD is
not leading you.

Dear Dreamer
Through adversity, GOD will birth some
qualities in you that you didn't know you
possessed. #Stand!

Dear Dreamer
There is FREEDOM in being who GOD has
called you to be.

Dear Dreamer
The door that GOD has for you is in your mouth.
speak the thing that you have been praying for…
and break FREE!

Dear Dreamer
GOD's plans will always be greater and
beautiful than all your disappointments.

Dear Dreamer
Live a HUMBLE life that pleases GOD not men.

Dear Dreamer
Choose PRINCIPLE over POPULARITY.

ABOUT THE AUTHOR

Determined, Innovative, Anointed, and Cutting Edge are some words often used to describe JERRY BONSU. Founder and Senior minister of Victory Life International Center (VLIC), a revolutionary Movement of 'like minded' and 'like spirited' people coming together in one accord: whose mission is to empower and equip individuals through teaching and preaching the uncompromised Word of God, and helping them to fulfill their highest calling and usher them into a supernatural lifestyle of faith and abundant living.

Jerry Bonsu is a visionary leader who merges multimedia, the marketplace, and faith into one dynamic calling. He is also the visionary and founder behind several entities, including: Victory in Praise International Gathering, a vibrant, dynamic worship conference, which brings together more than 2000 people each gathering, —a wide audience of pastors, worship leaders, artists, musicians, scholars, students, and other interested worshipers. Founder and President of Jerry Bonsu Ministries (JBM); Jerry is also the leader of a gospel group Jerry Bonsu & Levitical Anointing; And the co-founder of a non-profit organization Elyon Foundation, created to influence the next generation.

Jerry —dynamic conference speaker, author, life coach, entrepreneur, worship leader... also travels throughout the world with his breakthrough teaching on understanding your God-given identity, purpose, and destiny in Christ. His mission is to impact his generation with divine revelation. Jerry and his wife, Laetitia are the proud parents of two children, Janelle Kierra and Janessa Kimani.

Connect With Jerry!

Website: JerryBonsu.org
Speaking engagements: bookjerry@jerrybonsu.org
Facebook: Facebook.com/jerrybonsuministries
Instagram: Instagram.com/jerrybonsu
Twitter: Twitter.com/jerrybonsu
Youtube: Youtube.com/jerrybonsu
PUSH Conference: Jerrybonsu.org/Push
To join the mailing list: JerryBonsu.org

Books & CD's by Jerry Bonsu

* PUSH

* The Path to Victory

* Dear Dreamer

* God Is Up To Something Great

* The Broken Hearted

* The Power Of I AM

* The Power Of I AM (Audio Book)

* I AM Who God Says I AM
(Biblical Affirmations Book for Little Girls & Boys)

* Victory Noise (Album)

Grow deeper in your Christian Faith with a wide selection of CD'S & books written by **JERRY BONSU**
Visit jerrybonsu.org

Order these inspiring products and more by visiting
www.jerrybonsu.org and be sure to join us on Facebook,
Twitter & Instagram for more inspirational words.

WWW.JERRYBONSU.ORG

www.ingramcontent.com/pod-product-compliance
Lightning Source LLC
Chambersburg PA
CBHW071817020426
42331CB00007B/1513